The Story of the StarHearts™

With heartfelt appreciation
to my earthly StarHeart Angel Brigade—

Marlene, Dan, Izzy, Lillie,
Rick, Kandi, Jan & Dave,
Big Sis Sue & King Richard,
Dan the Star Gazin' Man,
My Mom

You have given me a galaxy of light and love.
Your encouragement to "reach for the moon"
is how this story finally "landed among the stars!"
Thank you so very much!

Cheryl Russell

Published by
Cheryl Russell
StarHeart Productions
Santa Ana, CA

Text Copyright © 1999
Illustrations Copyright © 2000
Trademark registered to Cheryl Russell

Design by Cheryl Russell
Illustrations by Dan Brouch
Graphic production by Kandi Gall

ISBN 0-9713181-0-7

All rights reserved. No part of this book may be reproduced or transmitted in any form or by any means, electronic or mechanical, including photocopying, recording, or by any information storage and retrieval system without permission in writing from the publisher.

Printed in Singapore

A long time ago . . .
it's difficult to say,

A universe was created—
it took more than a day.

This universe is special
with its galaxy of stars,

There is a planet called Earth
and another one called Mars.

This universe is unique
with two ingredients from above,

One is called "light"
the other is called "love".

Light comes from the heavens
the moon, the stars, the sun,

Being in the "light"
is such a lot of fun!

Love is in everything—
that means you and me,

It's in the plants and animals
even the fish in the sea!

No matter what it is
or where it may reside,

Everything has a heart
that can be found inside.

So if you think about it
and let your imagination go far,

You will have to agree
there's even a heart in every star.

StarHearts have been here
since the beginning of time,

Angels think they are magical
and they don't cost a dime.

Light and love
is what StarHearts are all about,

When you realize that power
it makes you want to shout!

Whenever you need comfort—
lots more love and light,

Just think about the StarHearts
and hold one very tight.

Healing is their greatest joy—
light and love is what it takes,

To relieve a scrape on the knee
or one of those awful tummy aches!

The power of StarHearts can help
whether the need is big or small,

There's a StarHeart Angel Brigade
that is very easy to call.

Just close your eyes gently—
picture as many angels as can be,

Keep them in your mind—
as many as you can see.

Before you know it
quick as a wink,

The StarHeart Angel Brigade
takes action before you can blink.

Hold on to a precious StarHeart
each time there is a need,

For light and love to lead the way
think StarHearts—YES, indeed!

About Cheryl Russell and Dan Brouch

Cheryl Russell is a "philosopher" who, in addition to her career in marketing communications, has shared her insights as a motivational speaker and writer for over 20 years. A native of southern California, she traveled solo around the world in 1980-81. Realizing this experience was more than a geographical journey, she wrote *The Art of Traveling, An Inspirational Guidebook*. She has written other books including *The Art of Saying "Thank You"...Why Gold Stars are So Important*.

The StarHearts began in 1995 as a logo for her quarterly newsletter, StarHeart Express—a publication that "speeds light and love your way." She wrote *The Story of the StarHearts* to explain her belief about the power that light and love have in our lives. As a further reminder, Cheryl has developed many gift items such as StarHeart stones, pillows, pins, calendars and note cards, as well as an activity-based workshop for children and adults called Camp StarHeart. For more information about her galaxy of StarHeart ideas contact:

Cheryl Russell
StarHeart Productions
(714) 436-1428

website: www.starheart.com
email: cheryl@starheart.com
Fax: (714) 546-4604

Dan Brouch is a freelance artist whose passion for drawing is apparent in every illustration. His whimsical art represents the experiences that have filled his life with inspiration. His art shines with color, as complex and vivid as the emotions that inspire them.

Dan has illustrated several picture books, as well as published many of his own fine works of art. He has recently finished writing and illustrating the first in a series of children's picture books filled with a colorful pallet of characters from within his own imagination. When he is not painting or drawing, he can usually be found somewhere on a beach along the coast in southern California, combing the shores for new ideas and inspiration.